The Silence of Goethe

Other works by Josef Pieper from St. Augustine's Press

The Concept of Sin

Death and Immortality

Enthusiasm and Divine Madness: On the Platonic Dialogue Phaedrus

Happiness and Contemplation

In Tune with the World: A Theory of Festivity

Scholasticism: Personalities and Problems of Medieval Philosophy

The Silence of St. Thomas: Three Essays

What Catholics Believe (with Heinz Kastop)

Tradition: Concept and Claim

Other titles of interest

C.S. Lewis and Don Giovanni Calabria, *The Latin Letters of C.S. Lewis*

Servais Pinckaers, O.P., *Morality: The Catholic View*

Peter Kreeft, *The Philosophy of Jesus*

Peter Kreeft, *Jesus-Shock*

Peter Kreeft, *The Sea Within: Waves and the Meaning of All Things*

Peter Kreeft, *I Surf, Therefore I Am: A Philosophy of Surfing*

Peter Kreeft, *If Einstein Had Been a Surfer: A Surfer, a Scientist, and a Philosopher Discuss a "Universal Wave Theory" or "Theory of Everything"*

Robert Hugh Benson, *Lord of the World*

James V. Schall, *The Regensburg Lecture*

Predrag Cicovacki, *Dostoevsky and the Affirmation of Life*

Nalin Ranasinghe, *Socrates in the Underworld: On Plato's* Gorgias

The Silence of Goethe

Josef Pieper

Preface by Ralph McInerny
Translated by Dan Farrelly

St. Augustine's Press
South Bend, Indiana
2009

Manufactured in the United States of America

1 2 3 4 5 6   14 13 12 11 10 09

Library of Congress Cataloging in Publication Data
Pieper, Josef, 1904–1997.
[Über das Schweigen Goethes. English]
The silence of Goethe / Josef Pieper;
translated by Dan Farrelly.
p. cm.
Includes bibliographical references and index.
ISBN-13: 978-1-58731-765-1 (hardbound: alk. paper)
ISBN-10: 1-58731-765-6 (pbk.: alk. paper)
ISBN-13: 978-1-58731-766-8 (hardbound: alk. paper)
ISBN-10: 1-58731-766-4 (pbk.: alk. paper)
1. Goethe, Johann Wolfgang von, 1749–1832.
I. Goethe, Johann Wolfgang von, 1749–1832. II. Title.
PT2054.P5313 2009
831'.6 – dc22   2009002334

∞ *The paper used in this publication meets the minimum
requirements of the American National Standard for
Information Sciences – Permanence of Paper for Printed
Materials, ANSI Z39.48-1984.*

ST. AUGUSTINE'S PRESS
www.staugustine.net

Men teach us to speak.
The gods teach us silence.

Plutarch

TABLE OF CONTENTS

Preface

JUST WHEN YOU MIGHT HAVE THOUGHT THAT ALL OF Josef Pieper is available in English and that our pleasure would consist only in rereading him, along comes *The Silence of Goethe*. It is a short book, but then all Pieper's books are short.

The poet said that *Obscurus fio dum brevis esse laboro: Obscurity besets me when I try for brevity.* Perhaps, as with many other German philosophers, length would have made Pieper obscure. In any case, brevity is his friend. *Leisure the Basis of Culture* was one of the earliest American paperbacks. Actually, it is two books: the title work and *Die philosophieren*, On philosophizing. Apparently the publisher thought that one alone would not be hefty enough. Recommended by T. S. Eliot, Pieper entered the American bloodstream and has been nourishing us ever sense.

Pieper was a speaker in a program I organized for the Department of Philosophy at Notre Dame many years ago, a program devoted to moral philosophy. The other participants were stellar figures, but Pieper was the superstar. It was his second visit to the university. He was as direct and apparently simple in lecturing as he is on the page. He is utterly un-Teutonic in being accessible to beginners. Is this simply popularizing? Philosophy for Dummies? (Why hasn't there been a Ventriloquism for Dummies?) Not at all. Just as a Socratic dialogue can be read by any reader and yet bring some back again and again for the 'more' that was missed before, so it with Pieper.

Pieper describes his first visit to Notre Dame in his autobiography; that was before my time. Many years after his participation in the program mentioned, I was asked to speak at Münster, an invitation I was glad to accept because of the prospect of seeing Josef Pieper again. He was too old to come to my talk – age has its rewards – so I visited him at his home.

A word picture. A vast sunken room, illumined by great windows looking out on a garden. Books everywhere. The philosopher rising from his desk and greeting one with oddly formal warmth. Scattered around the room are artifacts by his late wife. What did we talk about? Mutual friends, this and that. I recall no pearls of wisdom.

Yet in his presence I felt as I had in the presence of only a handful of other philosophers. Here was a man who deserved the title. Here was a lover of wisdom. He was retired then but one does not retire from loving wisdom. My colleague Otto Bird was another such personification of our profession.

The Münster professor who accompanied me to Pieper's home began early in the visit to suggest leaving. I ignored him, as did Pieper. When finally we did go, I learned that he had not been worried about tiring Pieper. He thought I would soon be bored by an old man's garrulity. Thus does proximity breed opacity. But then some found Socrates garrulous. *Quidquid recipitur ad modum recipientis recipitur.*

The Silence of Goethe opens with a tantalizing remark about how and where it got written. Toward the end of World War II, Pieper was imprisoned and took the occasion to read through the fifty volumes of Goethe's collected works. While this might sound like punishment to some, to Pieper it was an unlooked-for opportunity. And of course it suggests a not-altogether-menacing confinement. But then Boethius wrote *The Consolation of Philosophy* in prison.

Boethius' stay ended in execution, whereas Josef Pieper was released to half a century more of teaching and writing and lecturing.

Sooner or later, every German hopes to write about Goethe, nor does it usually take imprisonment in order for the hope to be realized. Pieper's perusal of the works of Germany's greatest writer produced a book that is vintage Pieper. He picks up on the reticence of Goethe. Think about that. A book about a poet, a novelist, a playwright, a political figure, producer of fifty volumes suggestive of any number of topics, and Pieper writes on Goethe's silence! Who other than Borges could surprise in that way?

Now I fall silent and turn you over to Josef Pieper.

Ralph McInerny

THE SILENCE OF GOETHE

THERE ARE, IT SEEMS, THINGS WHICH WORK OUT FOR US – no matter how much vigor is in our plans and intentions – only if we, as a friend used to say, are locked up for this specific purpose; if we, without any effort on our part, or through external force, are set free to deal with them. In this way a long-cherished plan came to fruition in a few glorious weeks. Through an almost magical stroke of good fortune I was plucked, as was Habakkuk, by the hair of his head and taken from the lethal chaos of the last months of the war, to be planted into a realm of the most peaceful seclusion, whose borders and exits were, of course, controlled by armed sentries.

But I was not locked away so completely that I could not succeed in making contact with a friend who lived quite close to that island. This proximity proved very fortunate – more so than anything I could ever have arranged for myself. Only a few days had passed and already a regular book-lending system was in full swing. This allowed me access to my friend's amazing treasures, and, after some sampling, I hit on the idea of asking not just for Goethe's letters but for the whole fifty volumes of the [Sophie] Weimar Edition, which were brought to me in sequence, two or three at a time, in a regular, mutual exchange.

The richness of this life revealing itself over a period of more than sixty years appeared before my gaze in its truly overpowering magnificence, which almost shattered my powers of comprehension – confined, as they had been, to the most immediate and pressing concerns. What a passionate focus on reality in all its forms, what an undying quest to chase down all that is in the world, what strength to affirm life, what ability to take part in it, what vehemence in the way he showed his dedication to it! Of course, too, what ability to limit himself to what was appropriate; what firm control in inhibiting what was purely aimless; what religious respect for the truth of being! I could not overcome my astonishment; and the prisoner entered a world without borders, a world in which the fact of being in prison was of absolutely no significance.

But no matter how many astonishing things I saw in these unforgettable weeks of undisturbed inner focus, nothing was more surprising or unexpected than this: to realize how much of what was peculiar to this life occurred in carefully preserved seclusion; how much the seemingly communicative man who carried on a world-wide correspondence still never wanted to expose in words the core of his existence. I had, of course, long since rid myself of the idea of finding the real Goethe in the host who was sought after by everyone, in the cheerful, many-sided conversationalist, or – in contrast to Schiller and even more so to Beethoven – the socially conforming courtier. But that this man, who in his advanced years said "that true happiness is really only to be found in sympathetic sharing,"[1] had become outstanding for his reticence – this insight, strange and all as it seems to me almost to this day, became established for me as a complete certainty only through that study.

IT IS BY NO MEANS THE CASE THAT THE MATURE GOE-
the, whose wisdom was based on a wide range of
human encounters, had thought of silence as a
last resort. Even at the age of twenty-seven, during the *Sturm und Drang* hustle and bustle of his
early Weimar period, he praises the hidden life as
the tried and tested, familiar shape that characterizes his own existence: "I am always living in a
crazy world and yet am very withdrawn within
myself."[2] "No one passing through, and hardly
anyone who lives here, would be able to say how
things really are with me; I have made up my
mind not to hear what people say about me."[3] In
1778 he writes to Charlotte von Stein that he is
beginning to fortify not just the castle but also the
town of his soul.[4] A good twenty years later he
takes up this image again in a letter to Schiller.
"The wall which I have erected around my existence should now be raised a couple of feet high-
er still."[5] This latter utterance of a fifty-year-old
man need not be seen as anything at all unusual.
But this continuo, which lasted for decades – and
began at such an early stage – made me see
Goethe, the person, in a new light. "In secret"

God gave him "rich blessings"; "for my fate is completely hidden from people. They can neither see nor hear anything of it."[6] "Deep down, in my plans, resolutions, and undertakings I remain secretly true to myself and tie together my social, political, moral, and poetic life in a hidden knot."[7] It is really a special and deliberate intention – here Goethe himself speaks, not quite seriously, of a "fault," though one which derives from his innermost nature – studiously aimed at "removing my existence, my actions, my writings from people's scrutiny."[8] "I was from early on convinced that one [should] go through the world either unknown or unidentified, so that on journeys, whether shorter or longer, I concealed my name as far as possible";[9] "thus in conversation with strangers or half strangers I will always . . . prefer the more insignificant subject or the less meaningful expression and in this way be interposed between myself and what I appear to be."[10] He could write to his son, when the Weimar court society was planning a gala production of *Götz* after the seventy-year-old had avoided birthday celebrations, "It has long been known and said that all personal involvement in the present is repugnant to me."[11] Sometimes it is as if he interrupted himself so that speech that was already taking

shape on his lips would fall silent again: "I spent
the evening filling several sheets of paper with the
description of my present situation; this morning,
when the messenger wants to collect it I can't
send it off. Our private burdens, our secret weak-
nesses and personal sufferings don't look very
well on paper" [this he wrote in 1810[12] to Duke
Carl August]; and a year earlier he wrote to Cotta
– it was a matter concerning "the dreadful state
of affairs regarding copyright and the lovely free-
dom of the press in Austrian territories" – : "I had
already composed a memorandum, the introduc-
tion and permission agreed, when, for better or
for worse, a spirit plucked at my sleeve and made
me think that it was not the right time to involve
myself in public affairs and that you live properly only if you lead a hidden life."[13]

The Silence of Goethe

HERE ONE CAN FIND, ACCORDING TO GOETHE HIMSELF, the key to many things. Once, twenty years before his death, the Princess of Solm-Braunfels presented him with a strange epitaph summing up and characterizing his life and work, saying he had a far greater need to penetrate into the innermost essence of man and concrete reality than to give poetic expression to his thoughts. Goethe said in reply that this statement, though true, astonished him. "If your Highness were to add: 'than to express himself by speaking, handing down, teaching, or doing,' then you have the key to much that must seem problematic about me and my life."[14] The gift of achieving anything through teaching is denied him, he writes to Schiller in 1797.[15]

So it is clear that he saw himself like this: "a magic oyster washed over by strange waves" [in a laconic later letter to Charlotte von Stein];[16] as one who has learned that "we and our ilk prosper only in stillness" [1816];[17] as "the hermit who, though in his cell, still hears the raging of the sea" [this is the conclusion of a letter to Sulpiz Boisserée a few years later[18]]; and at the age of eighty-one, when writing to Zelter, he calls himself "the lonely man who, like Merlin from his shining grave, let his own echo be heard, quietly and occasionally, both near and also in the distance."[19]

"What is best is the deep stillness" – after all that has gone before, this had to appear to me as a powerfully affirmed, secret [this too!] maxim of Goethe's existence, which he entrusted only to his diary – "What is best is the deep stillness in which, against the world, I live and grow, and gain what it cannot take from me by fire and sword."[20]

FOR THE MAN WHO LOVES QUIETNESS AND THE HIDDEN life to such an extent, silence becomes a habit: "I live in solitude, cut off from all company, which now finally makes me dumb as a fish."[21] "A person who is used to silence remains silent."[22] When I read this sentence in a letter to Charlotte von Stein I was suddenly reminded of an episode in *Kampagne in Frankreich*: during the retreat from France Goethe let himself, at a meal, be carried away to the point of "not entirely abstaining" from speaking of the past and of complaining about the catastrophic war situation and all the misery that followed from it. Thereupon his neighbor, a general, with impeccable correctness but also with a certain firmness, more or less called him to order; and then Goethe says: "I vowed inwardly to be in no hurry to break my customary silence again." "Almost a vow of silence," he says in 1784.[23] The seventy-five-year-old says: "I have trained myself not to speak about so-called maxims – to such an extent that none occur to me even in intimate company, to say nothing of larger gatherings."[24] But already when he was in Rome and Charlotte was beginning to distance herself from the man who fled to

Italy, Goethe writes to her: "There is still no letter from you and it seems to me ever more probable that your silence is intentional. I will accept this as well and reflect: after all, I have set the example for you, I have taught you to be silent."[25]

Here another side of Goethe's silence becomes apparent. Even this negative, fateful silence and need to be silent, which weighs on his soul like a curse, accompanied his existence – even, it seems, from early manhood until the end. How often, in the letters to Charlotte von Stein, do phrases like the following recur: "May a good spirit always keep my lips open."[26] Karl von Holtei has reported the seemingly not altogether infrequent "silent audiences,"[27] which were hardly less painful for the guest than for Goethe himself. And Zelter, worried, reproaches his aged friend with his "old malady": "brooding in isolation, consuming himself."[28]

But we should not see in this silence – even the less friendly silence – merely the gloom of a mind that is at odds with God and the world. There is also in it something of the resigned wisdom that characterizes the esoteric person. "I am often happy to record peculiar results of quiet, isolated thinking, and then I let go. This might eventually happen to all people if they arrive at the point where they cannot do without what is reasonable" – Goethe writes this a few months before his death.[29] And so even written expression seems too much for him – after he had, ten years previously, referred to the paradox of a reticent writer's existence in the beautiful sentence: "This is then the great charm of the otherwise questionable life of an author: that one is silent with one's friends and at the same time prepares a great conversation with them which reaches out to every part of the world."[30]

The one who knows does not speak – this sentence of Laotse could have been spoken by Goethe himself. A "secret society" really ought to be founded on art, he writes on one occasion to Schiller.[31] And he adopts the words of the scientist Peter Simon Pallas: "We academics should have kept the truth to ourselves."[32] "I have always thought it was bad, a misfortune that gained ground more and more in the second half of the previous century, that no distinction was made any more between the esoteric and the exoteric."[33] The insight of the observer and ponderer meets here with the innermost, fundamental tendency of the man who wishes to live his life "without noise"[34] "because I belong to those who themselves want to be left in peace and also don't want to stir up the people."[35] "To speak of a result that seems to be developing in me, it seems as if I like the idea of keeping my theories more and more to myself and revealing them less and less to others. People either joke or worry about life's riddles, but few are concerned with finding the solutions. Since they are all right in what they do, we should not confuse them."[36] The resignation in this latter formulation has a slightly contemptuous ring to it, which is characteristic of all esoterism. "Once the masses are satisfied with words and clichés they are not to be confused" – in these words to Zelter on 4 February 1832 the same characteristic is even more clearly evident. Of course there is no question of defending this, but on the other hand the price to be paid for the richness of this incomparable life is apparent. Goethe was glad "if a voice contradicts the jubilant applause that people express for actions and events which lead them to destruction";[37] but he himself did not want to be this voice.

Incidentally, regarding the remark about "contempt," there is need for a distinction. "In his attitude to the throng he uses irony." Who does? The *magnanimous*, the high-minded, the confident man who aims at greatness and tries to make himself worthy of it. Now this is not a

Goethean phrase. It is Aristotle or, more accurately, Thomas Aquinas. It is to be found in his *Commentary on Aristotle's Nicomachean Ethics*.[38] And it is certainly astounding that the "common teacher" of the as-yet-undivided Western Christendom should formulate such seemingly worldly philosophical thoughts. Not only is there no word of contradiction interpreting it, but furthermore, in the *Summa theologica* he has undertaken to defend it against the objection that contempt for people cannot be reconciled with humility. According to Thomas there is rightly contempt for all that is mean-spirited, and the bible text, "The villain is as nothing in his eyes," is applicable here. Such contempt is as little at odds with humility as it is at odds with truth, since no one's just claim to honor is being injured.[39]

GOETHE'S SILENCE IS IRONICAL IN THIS WAY WITH regard to his public. He wrathfully refuses to say what they want to hear: "If I had nothing to say except what pleases people, I would certainly say nothing, nothing at all."[40] One doesn't have to "engage with the public at all."[41] There can be no discussion with them. "By rights we know better what is good for the public than they do themselves. The citizens of a town can demand that the wells function and that sufficient water is there, but where it is to come from is a matter for the water management. In its ignorance, the public wants more and more water and often shuns the most productive sources; but you have to let them be, you say nothing, and you act according to your convictions."[42] That doesn't sound very democratic [no more than when, in Plato's dialogue,[43] Socrates interrupts Gorgias, the man who is successful in the eyes of the throng, with the words: "In the eyes of the throng – that is as much as to say 'in the eyes of the ignorant,' isn't it?"]. Without giving it a thought, Goethe presumes that his silence will be misunderstood by the many. He says of his liberalist indifference in religious matters that it only "appears" so, that

it is "only a mask behind which I sought to protect myself against pedantry and arrogance,"[44] a
mask of silence. But even with his closest and
dearest friends he remained silent about the most
exalted things. The manuscript of the last *Faust*
scenes came down to posterity sealed. No one
was to look up from these mystical verses and be
able to look into his eyes, questioning in astonishment, or even requiring answers.

Of course, when Goethe "likes to be silent
where there is talk of a divine Being," this comes
from roots which are even more hidden. In a letter of 9 June 1785 Goethe asks his friend Jacobi
for understanding.[45] To attempt a more penetrating interpretation would invite several questions,
including his self-characterization as "definitely a
non-Christian."[46] But there is certainly also a rev-
erent shyness at work, the same, which, in the
Summa theologica, gives rise to the first proposi-
tion in the theodicy: that we cannot say of God
what he is, but rather what he is not.[47] The experience of the "inadequacy of language," which is
"only a surrogate" has all too often – as we read
in a letter of Goethe's in March 1816 – prevented
him from "saying what I could and should have
said."[48] And this feeling does not seem to have
left this man – so much the master with words –

right to the end; indeed, it must have become
stronger: "Our best convictions cannot be
expressed in words. Language is not capable of
everything" – this is what we read in a letter written just under a week before his death.[49]

The Silence of Goethe

IN COMPARISON WITH SUCH SERIOUSNESS, THE SILENCE of the treasure-seeker seems almost playful. But, with a kind of superstition, Goethe took also this kind of silence seriously – right into his old age. "There is deep meaning in the mad notion that it is necessary to act in silence in order to raise and take possession of a treasure properly; it is not permitted to say one word, no matter how much that is shocking and delightful may appear on all sides."[50] He is about to write down for Schiller a plan for a new work when he claps his hand to his mouth: "Since I now know that I never finish anything if I confide my work plan in any way or have revealed it to someone, I prefer to hold back with this communication."[51] Almost one and a half decades later: "For usually, if I talk about something I don't do it."[52] And when the seventy-seven-year-old tells Sulpiz Boisserée, his friend from the Rhine, about Part Two of *Faust* – in a beautiful letter ["And complete in carefully measured days what you failed to do at a time when you have the right to believe or to suspect that there is another tomorrow or that there is always a tomorrow . . ."] – he stops: "Now that I read again what is here on the paper I ask myself whether I should send it. For we really ought not to speak of what we will do, of what we are doing, nor of what we have done."[53]

"See, dear friend, all that constitutes writing, its beginning and end, remains an eternal secret, thank God – something I am not prepared to reveal to the gapers and gossipers." It is after the creative storm which produced *Werther* that Goethe writes this to Jacobi.[54]

The Silence of Goethe

THE EXPERIENCE THAT "THE REPRODUCTION OF THE world around me by the inner world"[55] takes place in a cell to which no one else has entry makes him fall silent. From now on he knows that he must draw "a magic circle"[56] around himself, and "that I can only work in absolute isolation and that not only conversation, for instance, but even the domestic presence of dear and esteemed persons completely diverts my poetic sources."[57] "To wait in silence and to be concerned as little as possible about the public – this is what he found the soundest method of dealing with difficulties in mastering his material."[58]

People of average education, not identifying themselves with the public, find it easy to forgive such pronounced distance from the public; yet it is well known that Goethe is blamed for taking such little interest in the political happenings of his day; that *Reineke Fuchs* was written "to distract me from thinking about events in the world – and with success";[59] and that the sixty-four-year-old, on the eve of the decisive battle of 1813, obstinately threw himself "into the remotest of things" and devoted himself "to the most serious study of the Chinese empire"[60] – this, too, a form of silence. It is not the aim of this modest report to defend or to explain. But one must not overlook this particular silence of Goethe which in the most recent past has often been censured (or passionately denied). Only in those weeks of captivity did I myself realize how much this is one of many manifestations of the same attitude. – The publisher Perthes calls on him to collaborate on the periodical *Vaterländisches Museum*. Goethe's answer: "I have every reason to be focused if I am to cope to some extent with my obligations. And then we are living in an age where I like to let time pass a little if I am to speak to it or about it."[61] "My obligations": the same 16 November 1810 date on this letter of refusal to Perthes is found on the letter to another publisher, Cotta, in which his plan for *Dichtung und Wahrheit* is sketched! So, escape from his time? "I would really like to take part in our time," another letter says to the younger Schlegel a year-and-a-half later. There is no reason to see in this an inaccurate account of himself. Of course, the sentence that follows must not be ignored: "I would really like to take part in our time, but I am not sure how to handle it if I am to live with it; that's why you will find me seldom – or not at all – appearing in publications

which are devoted to the present."[62] Certainly in
communicating with his more intimate friends he
uses much stronger words, and his references to
gazettes and journals are not exactly friendly. "I
have no rapport with daily, weekly, and monthly
publications. These have a bad way of using the
loftiest words – which should only be used to
express the best things – as trite phrases to mask
what is mediocre or even less. In such company
a definite sensible word does not have its right
effect" – this he writes to Sulpiz Boisserée.[63] And
even more in the letters to Zelter! "You see that I
don't need to occupy myself with the daily
papers" – no, I must quote the wonderful passage
in this letter in full. It is necessary to keep the
deep "inner calm at sea," out of which, in his
very last years, precisely the letters to Zelter are
written ["Now that I have found out that the
whole of Europe, leveled by a blanket of snow just
like my cloister garden, has to cope, I too have to
manage, all the more so since I am not called
upon to put my foot outside the door. And so, in
the clear sky at night, where Lady Venus, still
cheerful and sweet, shines in the western sky
over the horns of the new moon, then Orion and
his dog, with twinkling collar, rises gloriously from
the east over my dark spruce horizon, excited by

all this I want to send a warm and cheerful word to you in your well-lit and busy town."].[64] But the entire passage about the "daily papers" – Goethe is writing from the bay window directly overlooking the Camsdorf Saale bridge in Jena – is as follows: "I am again standing at my vantage point over the water rushing under the bridge; the fine logs, joined together in twos, travel through circumspectly and happily down the stream. One man performs the task adequately, the second one is there only as if to keep him company. The logs of firewood follow merrily behind, some coming down the stream like the longer ones, others of them driven swirling around as God chooses, others driven for a time onto the shingle and the sandbank. Perhaps tomorrow the water will rise, lift them all, and lead them for miles to their destination, the fire-place. You can see that I don't need to occupy myself with the daily papers, since the most perfect symbols happen before my very eyes."[65] Zelter was also the one to whom Goethe, several months earlier, had spoken of the "foolish noise of our daily papers" which made him feel as if he had learned to fall asleep in a mill and heard and knew nothing about it.[66] And again it is Zelter to whom, a dozen years later, he confides the "amazing fact . . .

that, after I make a quick and strict resolution, I have done away with all reading of newspapers."[67]

There are still many facets to Goethe's silence that one could report. It is not easy to exhaust the study of all aspects. One would have, for instance, to speak of the silence of the man who is all too vulnerable; a word would be needed about the loyalty of the man who, with regard to shortcomings of friends, maintains an inner silence, a silence imposed on himself. Friedrich Wilhelm Riemer relates how Goethe never passed judgment "about his friends and persons he loved. 'I don't think about them,' he said when someone wanted to tell him about their qualities and peculiarities."[68] One must also contemplate the wise economy – which has nothing at all to do with a selfish form of comfort – that makes him simply ignore the negative and pass over it in silence as if it did not exist. In one of his first letters to Charlotte von Stein this wisdom is already formulated like a principle. "Of all the things on earth that can be harmful and lethal to me, annoyance is the least. Of course there is never any lack of reasons for it; it is just that I don't bother with it."[69] And twenty-two years later: "The practical man, when he is young, does well to take no notice of his opponents."[70] And twenty years later: "I am saying nothing about our internal affairs. I even ignore them here on the spot. I know nothing that spoils my day more than such faction gossip."[71] The culmination is when the eighty-year-old sees forgetting not as a convulsive refusal to think of things, but as what could almost be termed a physiological process of simple forgetting as a function of life. He praises as "a great gift of the gods" . . . "the ethereal stream of forgetfulness" which he "was always able to value, to use, and to heighten."[72]

HOWEVER MANIFOLD THE FORMS OF THIS SILENCE AND of their unconscious roots and conscious motives may have been, is it not always the possibility of hearing, the possibility of a purer perception of reality that is aimed at? And so, is not Goethe's type of silence above all the silence of one who listens? And his seeming lack of interest, the fact that he is easily disturbed, even his occasional moody irritability – are these not the sensitivity of one who is hindered by fuss and noise from hearing what he considers to be genuine reality [just as the dismissive gesture, as it were pointing to the door, is part of the language characteristic of the intense listener]? "Gently, gently" to unfold the problems like layers of an onion and "to retain respect for all truly, quietly living buds" – this is his "old and tried method." Is that not said about someone who wants only to hear and listen? And the unbelievable continuity is astonishing. A sentence written to Charlotte von Stein almost exactly a half-century earlier corresponds completely to the sentence to Zelter[73] just quoted: "Since I am now inwardly as pure and still as the air, the breath of good and quiet people is very welcome to me."[74]

This listening silence is much deeper than the mere refraining from words and speech in human intercourse. It means a stillness, which, like a breath, has penetrated into the inmost chamber of one's own soul. It is meant, in the Goethean "maxim," to "deny myself as much as possible and to take up the object into myself as purely as it is possible to do." This listening silence, which is open – deep into the inner self – to the language of existing things is what is meant when the traveler in Italy reports to Herder from Rome how he is exercising himself "in seeing and reading all things as they are"; "this exercise," Goethe writes, "and my fidelity in letting my eye see freely, my complete renunciation of all pretension are here giving me great happiness in quietude."[75]

The Silence of Goethe

THE MEANING OF BEING SILENT IS HEARING – A HEARING in which the simplicity of the receptive gaze at things is like the naturalness, simplicity, and purity of one receiving a confidence, the reality of which is *creatura*, God's creation. And insofar as Goethe's silence is in this sense a hearing silence, to that extent it has the status of the model and paradigm – however much, in individual instances, reservations and criticism are justified. One could remain circumspectly silent about this exemplariness after the heroic nihilism of our age has proclaimed the attitude of the knower to be by no means that of a silent listener but rather as that of self-affirmation over against being: insight and knowledge are naked defiance, the severest endangering of existence in the midst of the superior strength of concrete being. The resistance of knowledge opposes the oppressive superior power. However, that the knower is not a defiant rebel against concrete being, but above all else a listener who stays silent and, on the basis of his silence, a hearer – it is here that Goethe represents what, since Pythagoras, may be considered the silence tradition of the West.

A particular form of not being silent has been understood, since time immemorial, as brother to despair: *verbositas*, talk, chatter, the ceaseless activity of simply making words.[76] Since time immemorial – that can be said. This link is to be found in the writings of Cassian, a famous monk of the fifth century. Others are Gregory the Great, Isidore of Seville, and Thomas Aquinas. Similarly, the link is found in the analysis of "daily existence," which is one of the lasting discoveries of Martin Heidegger. Also in the dark book of the *Christian Epimetheus* left to us by the poet Konrad Weiß, the concrete form of that not being silent is brought before our eyes in an exact and rich utterance. He speaks of the many people who have time to discuss things helplessly – with faces characterized by worry – "and whose curiosity (the kind that wants to find satisfaction in daily things) amounts to avoiding disappointment rather than hoping. It is that expression of a face, which, focused on a concrete thing, does not enjoy the quiet fulfillment of further certainties that are not of a political nature."[77]

xxxxWhen such talk, which one encounters absolutely everywhere in workshops and in the marketplace – and as a constant temptation – , when such deafening talk, literally out to thwart listening, is linked to hopelessness, we have to ask is there not in silence – listening silence – necessarily a shred of hope? For who could listen in silence to the language of things if he did not expect something to come of such awareness of the truth? And, in a newly founded discipline of silence, is there not a chance not merely to overcome the sterility of everyday talk but also to overcome its brother, hopelessness – possibly if only to the extent that we know the true face of this relationship? I know that here quite different forces come into play which are beyond human control, and perhaps the *circulus* has to be broken through in a different place. However, one may ask: could not the "quick, strict resolution" to remain silent at the same time serve as a kind of training in hope?

ENDNOTES TO *THE SILENCE OF GOETHE*

The introductory quotation from Plutarch is taken from the treatise on "Talkativeness," ch. 8. See Plutarch, *Moralia* (*Sammlung Dieterich*, 1942), p. 148.

1   To Sarah von Grotthuß, 23 April 1814
2   To J.H. Merck, 5 January 1777
3   To J.G. Zimmermann, 6 March 1776
4   From Berlin, 17 May 1778: "The gods preserve my equanimity and purity extremely well, but, against that, the bloom of trust, openness, and loving surrender is fading more every day. My soul was once a city with low walls with a citadel behind it on the mountain. I guarded the castle and I left the city without defenses in peace and in war. Now I am beginning to fortify it."
5   27 July 1779
6   To J.K. Lavater, 8 October 1779
7   To K.L. von Knebel, 21 November 1782
8   To Schiller, 9 July 1796
9   To J.H. Meyer, 30 December 1795

10 To Schiller, 9 July 1796

11 To August von Schiller, 18 October 1819: "It is long since established that any personal dealings are extremely repugnant to me at present. Please make the point in a courteous and friendly way."

12 7 May 1819

13 1 October 1809

14 3 January 1812

15 12 August 1797

16 8 March 1808

17 To Christian T. von Voigt, 27 February 1816

18 16 July 1820

19 14 December 1830

20 Diary entry "in the garden house," 13 May 1780

21 To F.H. Jacobi, 14 April 1786

22 20 December 1786 from Rome

23 To Duke Carl August, 26 December 1784

24 To C.L.F. Schultz, 3 July 1824

25 20 December 1786

26 29 December 1786, from Rome

27 *Goethe's Conversations, excluding those with Eckermann: A Selection*, edited by Flodoard Freiherr von Biedermann, Leipzig (Insel-Verlag: n.d.), no. 414 (beginning of May 1827).

28 "I think of you a prey to your old ailment – lonely, brooding, eating your heart out." Zelter to Goethe, 21–23 April 1806.

29 To K.F. Zelter, 1 June 1831

30 To K.F. Zelter, 18 February 1821

31 14 January 1801

32 To Passow, 20 October 1811

33 ibid.

34 To Charlotte von Stein, 1 December 1807

35 To F.H. Jacobi, 10 May 1812

36 To Schiller, 12 July 1801

37 To Joh. von Müller, 2 July 1782

38 "Utitur autem ironia in societate multorum." Thomas Aquinas, *Commentary on the Nicomachean Ethics of Aristotle*, book 4, lectio 10.

39 *Summa theologica* II-II, 129, 3 and 4

40 To C.L.F. Schultz, 8 June 1818

41 To Schiller, 7 November 1798

42 To H.K.A. Eichstädt, 23 January 1805

43 *Gorgias* 459

44 In Goethe's *Tag- und Jahreshefte*, for the year 1807, there is mention of the meeting in Carlsbad with the Royal Saxon Chief Court Preacher Reinhard: "His fine moral nature, his cultivated mind, his honest intentions, and his practical insight into what is desirable and worth striving for – these were all apparent in this venerable and kindly man. Although he could not quite accept my way of commenting on whatever confronted me, I was still happy to see that I was

in complete agreement with him on some important points while in conflict with current opinion. He was able to see from this that my apparent liberal indifference – on the most serious level in accord with him for practical purposes – was only a mask behind which I sought to protect myself on other occasions against pedantry and arrogance.

45   J.F. Rochlitz reports [see *Gedenk-Ausgabe of the Artemis-Verlag*, vol. 22 (1949), pp. 716ff.] a "long, very serious and penetrating conversation" he had with Goethe, in which he, Rochlitz, was finally tired and exclaimed, "quite unintentionally": "I would have thought: enough for today! And let us just give honor to God and loudly proclaim his moral world regime." Whereupon Goethe suddenly stood still and said "in a solemn tone": "Proclaim? It? Who would not have to! But I do it in silence. . . . Who can express it, except of course to himself? To others – who? And if he knows that he cannot, then he is not permitted to do it."

46   To J.K. Lavater, 29 July 1782

47   *Summa theologica*, I, 3, prooemium

48   To C.L.F. Schultz, 11 March 1816

49   To Count K. von Sternberg, 15 March 1832

50   *Tag- und Jahreshefte*, for the year 1803, at the beginning of the section

51   28 April 1797

52   To K.F. von Reinhard, 8 May 1811

53   22 October 1826

54   21 August 1774

55   ibid.

56   To Duke Carl August [from Rom], 8 December 1787

57   To Schiller, 9 December 1797

58   To K.L. von Knebel, 16 July 1798

59   To F.H. Jacobi, 2. May 1793

60   "Here I must mention another peculiarity of my way of behaving. When some monstrous threat emerges in the political sphere, I stubbornly throw myself into something extremely remote from it. An example of this is that, from the time of my return from Carlsbad, I dedicated myself to the serious study of the Chinese Empire, and, in between, with an unavoidable and unpleasant performance of *Essex* in mind – to please the actress and to give a bit of luster to her unfortunate role – I wrote the epilogue to *Essex on the very day of the Battle of the Nations.*" *Tag- und Jahreshefte* fr the year 1813

61   16 November 1810

62   To Friedrich von Schlegel, c. 8 April 1812

63   26 June 1811

64   29 January 1830

65 19 March 1818

66 31 December 1817

67 29 April 1830

68 Fr. W. Riemer, *Mitteilungen über Goethe*, ed. Arthur Pollmer, Leipzig [Insel-Verlag], 1921, pp. 143ff.

69 20 March 1776

70 To Schiller, 28 July 1798

71 To Sulpiz Boisserée, 1 May 1818

72 To K.F. Zelter, 15 February 1830

73 9 November 1829

74 End of September 1779 [visit to Sesenheim]

75 10 & 11 November 1786

76 For more detail, see Josef Pieper, *Über die Hoffnung*, Munich, 6th edition, 1961 [chapter on "Verzweiflung"].

77 Konrad Weiß, *Der Christliche Epimetheus*, Berlin, 1933, p. 92

Excerpts from Goethe's Letters

1

A person who has [riches] may not bless. He must give. But if the great and wealthy of this world hand out property and titles, fate has given the poor man, as a counter-balance, a blessing in which the fortunate man sees nothing to attract his greed.

2

The greatest people whom I have known and whose view of heaven and earth was not obscured, were humble and knew the scale of values they had to use.

3

What a person must do allows him to show what he is inwardly like. Anyone can live arbitrarily.

4

Furthermore, fairness and tolerance in taste is hardly a distinguishing feature of a king, no more

than it, if he had it, would earn him a great repu-
tation. I am more inclined to think the ability to
exclude is what characterizes the great and dis-
tinguished.

5

One thing remains certain: this public, so hon-
ored and despised, is almost always wrong about
the details and almost never wrong about the
totality.

6

The soul will be brought ever more deeply back
to itself the more we treat people according to
what they are rather than according to what suits
us.

7

Children are a real touchstone of what is false-
hood and what is truth. They have far less need
for self-deception than do old people.

8

Since peace can be the only reason for war, it is
more fitting for the warrior to make peace – and
keep it – without war.

9

We can do no more than build a stack of wood and dry it properly. Then it will catch fire at the right time and we ourselves will be astonished by it.

10

It always seems to me that if one speaks of writings and deeds without loving sympathy, without a certain biased enthusiasm, so little is left that it is hardly worth talking about. Pleasure, joy, participation in things are all that is real and that then produces reality. Anything else is futile and has a frustrating effect.

11

We don't believe how much is dead and deadly in the sciences until we ourselves become seriously and energetically involved in them. And I am convinced that the spirit that drives really scientific people is sophistry rather than a love of truth.

12

Our links with the external world make up our existence and rob us of it at the same time, and yet we have to find a way to manage.

13

My resolute hatred of rapturous enthusiasm, hypocrisy, and presumption often used to make me unjust also towards the true, ideal good in people that cannot be shown in experience in a completely pure form. Time teaches us about this as about many another thing, and we learn that true appreciation is not possible without making allowances.

14

All business is like marriage. We are amazed at our achievement in tying the knot, and now all hell breaks loose. That is because nothing in the world exists in isolation, and whatever is effective must be seen not as an end but as a beginning.

15

In scrutinizing the way things have gone for me and others, in life and art, I often found that what one rightly calls a false striving is for the individual a completely necessary detour to one's goal. Every turning back from error has a powerful formative influence on a person's development, both in particular and in general, so that it is easy to understand how the searcher of hearts can prefer one sinner to the ninety-nine just.

Excerpts from Goethe's Letters

16

When all bonds are dissolved, we have to fall back on the domestic ones.

17

And so, while I look at them, the mistakes dissolve into good. It is the same with observing individuals in whom we are always finding things to praise and blame and whom, in the end, we have to love anyway. The synthesis wrought by affection is what brings everything to life.

18

Educated people and those who work at the education of others spend their lives without noise.

19

Older acquaintances and friendships have the advantage over new ones in that much has already been forgiven.

20

I have noticed repeatedly, from my isolated vantage point, that it is not possible to write world history by adopting a moral stance.

21

Every genuine artist is to be seen as one who

wants to preserve something acknowledged as holy and to propagate it with deep seriousness and thought. But every century strives in its own way towards the secular and seeks to make what is holy common, what is weighty light, and what is serious funny. There is nothing to be said against this as long as it doesn't result in destroying both seriousness and fun.

22

Meanwhile it seems strange to me that science, which in its veiled origins begins as a secret, must become a secret again in its infinite unfolding.

23

People become united in their mental attitudes and are separated by their opinions. The former are simple and bring us together; the latter are manifold and scatter us. Friendships in our youth are based on the former and the latter are blamed for divisions in later life. If we were aware of this earlier, we would, while forming our own way of thinking, soon form a more liberal view of the other – even of the opposite mode. In this way we would be more conciliatory and, through our mental attitude, seek to gather together again what opinions have split up.

Excerpts from Goethe's Letters

I will state here my
general confession of faith:

a. In nature, all that is in the subject is
y and something more.
b. In the subject, all that is in nature is
z and something more

b. can know a.,
but y can only be sensed through z.

This is where equilibrium of the world originates, along with the circle of life to which we are assigned. The being that encompasses all four with the highest degree of clarity has been called God by all races since time immemorial.

25
Idea and experience will never meet in the middle. They can only be unified through art and action.

26
The best judgment is the only one which you pass on your productions after a number of years when, through further education, you have surpassed them.

27

Although because of my way, good or bad, I was never capable of applying sufficient diligence to being correct and clearly organized, still I have come to understand clearly that language is only a surrogate, whether what we want to express is preoccupying us inwardly or is stimulating us externally. On the way, I have become only too aware of this inadequacy of language and have thereby let myself be held back from saying what I could and should have said.

28

Internally one must not deviate – not even by a hair's breadth – from the highest maxims of art and life, but in the empirical world, in the bustle of the day, I prefer to accept something of moderate standard than to pass over the good in it or carp at it.

29

Every century has its grimace.

30

Everything that happens is symbol, and when presenting itself perfectly it indicates the rest.

31

If I had nothing to say except what people want to hear, I would be completely silent.

32

Faith, love, and hope are the basis of the religion, art, and science of the man favored by God. These latter nourish and satisfy the need to show adoration, to produce, to see. All three are one, from the beginning and at the end, although separated in the middle.

33

There are three kinds of reader: one who enjoys without making a judgment, a third who judges without enjoyment, and, in the middle, one who judges while enjoying and enjoys while judging. This middle one reproduces a work of art anew.

34

The snipe of life whizzes by. A good marksman must take it quickly.

35

If to understand means to find within oneself what another has said, women, where it is a question of inward things, have the advantage.

36

The individual has to give an account of himself.
No one comes to his aid.

37

I can well maintain that every bad thing, the
worst thing we meet within the law – of whatever
kind: natural or civil, bodily or economic – is not
equal to a thousandth of the wrongs we have to
grapple with if we act outside the law, side by side
with it, or cutting across law and tradition, and at
the same time feel the need to retain equilibrium
with ourselves, with others, and with world order.

38

The good judge of human nature should admit to
himself that no one is convinced by his oppo-
nent's fundamental reasons. All arguments are
only variations of an initial, firmly rooted opinion. For this reason our forefathers so wisely said:
don't argue with someone who denies your prin-
ciples.

39

What would be the reason for our activity if every
person did not overvalue himself to some extent
and try to shut the circle around him?

Excerpts from Goethe's Letters

40

We know quite well that the human being has to draw everything to himself – even God and the divine – and to assimilate it. But there are grades of this: high and ordinary.

41

I have never made a secret of the fact that I am a deadly enemy of all parody and travesty. But this is only so because this horrible breed drags down the beautiful, the noble, and the great in order to destroy it. I don't even like to see mere appearances banished by it.

42

With every separation we feel what sated presence conceals.

43

Just as the feeling of misfortune is alleviated by time so also is happiness much in need of this beneficial influence.

44

True originality is at work where there is need only of an impulse to stir it up, and then of itself and quite independently it is able to follow the path of the true, the solid, and the durable.

45

We concede that there are problems everywhere and yet we cannot let any of them alone. And this is quite right, for otherwise research would stop. But with positive things we shouldn't take it too seriously but use irony to stand above everything. In this way the specific quality of the problem is retained.

46

We like to think of life in connection with death – not as night, but as eternal day where death is always swallowed up by life.

47

We should, in good time, tell ourselves that it is advisable to avoid what we cannot enjoy assimilating, or what we cannot engage in productively, bringing joy to ourselves and others.

48

Il faut croire à la simplicité! In translation: If we are to find the right way we have to believe in simplicity, in the simple, in what is the fundamental basis of the productive. This is, however, not granted to everyone. We are born in an artificial condition, and it is much easier to cultivate this artificiality than to return to basic simplicity.

49

So I still say that the spirit of reality is in fact the truly ideal. We should not spurn the directly visible world of the senses, for otherwise we travel without ballast.

50

Much remains unknown to the world; what is known is forgotten by posterity; narrow-minded contemporaries and an arrogant new generation obscure and obliterate years of fruitful endeavor, until finally historical interest, possibly to be described as a restless belated curiosity, knows no end to its inquiries about memoirs, diary notes, letters, and other scraps of paper.

51

True conviction comes from the heart. The soul [Gemüt], where conscience really resides, judges about what is admissible and inadmissible much more reliably than the intellect, which will sometimes see and decide without going to the heart of the matter.

52

There is a delicate empirical approach which achieves intimate identity with the object and in this way arrives at proper theory. But this heightening of our spiritual capacity belongs to a highly cultivated era.

53

Truth is simple and gives rise to little activity. What is false occasions the splitting of time and energy into fragments.

54

I have resurrected the old truth: that just as nature and poetry have perhaps never been so intimately integrated in the modern period as in Shakespeare, the highest culture and poetry have never been more intimately integrated than in Calderón.

55

Consider: every single idea makes its appearance as a foreign guest and, as it begins to be realized, is hardly distinguishable from fantasy and the fantastic.

56

Nothing diverts me from my tried and tested

method: gently to unveil the problems, gently as we remove layers of an onion, and to retain respect for all truly, quietly living buds. The older I become the more confidence I have in the law that governs the way roses and lilies bloom.

57

Consider that with every breath our whole being is penetrated by an ethereal stream of forgetfulness, so that we have a moderate memory of our joys and hardly any memory of our sufferings. I have always been able to prize this great divine gift, to use it and to heighten it. So, when it is a question of the blows and jolts with which our lovers, friends, and enemies have tried us, for the good and resolute person the memory of these things has long since disappeared into the air.

58

To see people and things exactly as they are and to say exactly what is on our mind – this is the right thing. We should not and cannot do more.

59

It is quite astonishing that we feel these irresistible urges to practice things in which we can have no success and yet are thereby helped, in a very real way, to achieve the things of which we really are capable.

60

In science I have been hearing during my whole life, on the occasions when something significant has been produced: what is true in it is not new, and what is new in it is not true. That means no more than: what we have learned we think we understand, and what we ought to learn we don't understand.

61

I am indebted to critical and idealistic philosophy for making me reflect on myself, which is an enormous gain; but it never attains to the object. Along with ordinary common sense we have to acknowledge the object if, in our unchanging relationship to it, we are to experience the joys of living.

62

We must realize the need to suppose and believe that what we have seen and known as simple reality is part of something complex. For the simple is hidden in multiplicity, and that is where, for me, faith comes into it: faith is not the beginning but the end of all knowledge.

63

The most wonderful thing is that the best of our convictions cannot be expressed in words. Language is not adequate for everything, and often we are not quite sure whether, in the end, we are seeing, looking, thinking, remembering, fantasizing, or believing.

ENDNOTES FOR EXCERPTS FROM GOETHE'S LETTERS

The sequence of the texts corresponds to the chronological sequence of the letters.

1   To J.F. Krafft, 23 November 1778
2   To J.K. Lavater, end of July 1781
3   To J.F. Krafft, 31 January 1781
4   To Jenny von Voigts, 21 June 1781
5   To Charlotte von Stein, 10 December 1781
6   To Charlotte von Stein, 13 May 1782
7   To Charlotte von Stein, 5 October 1784
8   To Duke Carl August, February 1790
9   To Schiller, 28 February 1795
10 To Schiller, 14 June 1796
11 K.L. von Knebel, 12 January1798
12 To Schiller, 19 June 1799
13 To F.H. Jacobi, 2 January 1800
14 To Schiller, 5 July 1802
15 To H.K.A Eichstädt, 15 September 1804
16 To Duke Carl August, 25 December 1806
17 To K.F. von Reinhard, 28 August 1807
18 To Charlotte von Stein, 1 December 1807

19 To Dorothea von Knabenau, 14 October 1808
20 To K.F. von Reinhard, 22 July 1810
21 To K.F. Zelter, 18 March 1811
22 To Th.J. Seebeck, 29 April 1812
23 To F.H. Jacobi, 6 January 1813
24 To C.H. Schlosser, 19 February 1815
25 To Arthur Schopenhauer, 28 January 1816
26 To Teuscher, 28 January 1816
27 To C.L.F. Schultz, 11 March 1816
28 To K.F. Zelter, 7 November 1816
29 To Christian G. von Voigt, 18 June 1817
30 To C.E. Schubarth, 2 April 1818
31 To C.L.F. Schultz, 8 June 1818
32 To C.E. Schubarth, 21 April 1819
33 To F. Rochlitz, 13 June 1819
34 To Sulpiz Boisserée, 16 July 1820
35 To K.F.A von Conta, 25 September 1820
36 To C.L.F. Schultz, 24 September 1821
37 To C.E. Schubarth, 7 November, 1821
38 To C.F. Bachmann, 2 February 1822
39 To Count K. von Sternberg, 2 August, 1822
40 To K.F. Zelter, 24 July 1823
41 To K.F. Zelter, 26 June 1824
42 To J.J. von Willemer, 6 October 1824
43 To C.E.A. von Hoff, 4 December 1825
44 To J.E. Purkinje, 18 March 1826
45 To Count K. von Sternberg, 26 September 1826
46 To Christian G.D. Nees von Esenbeck, 27 September 1826

INDEX TO *THE SILENCE OF GOETHE*

INDEX TO EXCERPTS FROM GOETHE'S LETTERS

Entries in this index are by Excerpt, not page number; Names listed are recipients of Goethe's letters.

science, has much that is dead and deadly, 11; begins as secret and must become a secret again to unfold, 22
scientific people are driven by sophistry rather than love of truth, 11
see and say what is true, 58
Seebeek, Th.J., 22
self-(over)value is basis for activity, 39
senses, not to be spurned, 49
separation opens what presence conceals, 42
Shakespeare, epitome of integration of nature and poetry, 54
silence, necessary if one has nothing to say except what people want to hear, 31
simple, what appears simple is part of something complex, 62
simplicity, leads to productive life, but is hard to cultivate, 48
Sömmering, S.Th. von, 50
soul, made more itself by treating people according

to the truth rather than what suits us, 6; s. judges more reliable than the intellect, 51
speech, reticence in, necessitated by its being a surrogate and inadequate, 27
Stein, Charlotte von, 5–7, 18
Sternberg, Count K. von, 39, 45, 63
subject, know this first, then acknowledge the subject to experience the joys of life, 61
symbol, everything happens is s., 40
sympathy, as making life worthwhile, 10

Teuscher, Ch.F.G., 26
time, alleviates feeling of misfortune and promotes happiness, 43
tolerance comes from making allowances and overcoming emotion, 13
truth, simple and gives rise to little activity, whereas the false is very active, 53